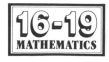

Modelling with force and motion

Unit guide

The School Mathematics Project

CAMBRIDGE
UNIVERSITY PRESS

Main authors	Stan Dolan
	Judith Galsworthy
	Mike Hall
	Janet Jagger
	Ann Kitchen
	Paul Roder
	Tom Roper
	Mike Savage
	Bernard Taylor
	Carole Tyler
	Nigel Webb
	Julian Williams
	Phil Wood
Team leader	Ann Kitchen
Project director	Stan Dolan

Many others have helped with advice and criticism.

This unit has been produced in collaboration with the Mechanics in Action Project, based at the Universities of Leeds and Manchester.

The authors would like to give special thanks to Ann White for her help in producing the trial edition and in preparing this book for publication.

Published by the Press Syndicate of the University of Cambridge
The Pitt Building, Trumpington Street, Cambridge CB2 1RP
40 West 20th Street, New York, NY 10011–4211, USA
10 Stamford Road, Oakleigh, Victoria 3166, Australia

© Cambridge University Press 1992

First published 1992

Produced by Gecko Limited, Bicester, Oxon.

Cover design by Iguana Creative Design

Printed in Great Britain at the University Press, Cambridge

British Library cataloguing in publication data

A catalogue record for this book is available from the British Library.

ISBN 0 521 40883 0

Contents

Structure of the courses

The A and AS level courses have a core-plus-options structure. Details of the full range of possibilities, including A and AS level *Further Mathematics* courses, may be obtained from the Joint Matriculation Board, Manchester M15 6EU.

For the A level course *Mathematics (Pure with Applications)*, students must study eight core units and a further two optional units. The structure diagram below shows how the units are related to each other. Other optional units are presently being developed to give students an opportunity to study aspects of mathematics which are appropriate to their personal interests and enthusiasms.

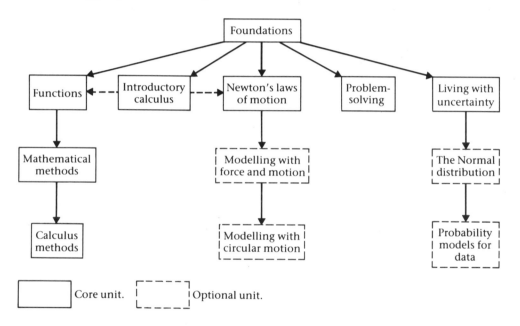

The *Foundations* unit should be started before or at the same time as any other core unit.

Any of the other units can be started at the same time as the *Foundations* unit. The second half of *Functions* requires prior coverage of *Introductory calculus*. *Newton's laws of motion* requires calculus notation which is covered in the initial chapters of *Introductory calculus*.

For the AS level *Mathematics (Pure with Applications)* course, students must study *Foundations*, *Introductory calculus* and *Functions*. Students must then study a further two applied units.

Material

In traditional mathematics texts the theory has been written in a didactic manner for passive reading, in the hope that it will be accepted and understood – or, more realistically, that the teacher will supply the necessary motivation and deal with problems of understanding. In marked contrast, *16–19 Mathematics* adopts a questing mode, demanding the active participation of students. The textbooks contain several new devices to aid a more active style of learning.

- Topics are opened up through **group discussion points**, signalled in the text by the symbol

and enclosed in rectangular frames. These consist of pertinent questions to be discussed by students, with guidance and help from the teacher. Commentaries for discussion points are included in this unit guide.

- The text is also punctuated by **thinking points**, having the shape

and again containing questions. These should be dealt with by students without the aid of the teacher. In facing up to the challenge offered by the thinking points it is intended that students will achieve a deeper insight and understanding. A solution within the text confirms or modifies the student's response to each thinking point.

- At appropriate points in the text, students are referred to **tasksheets** which are placed at the end of the relevant chapter. A tasksheet usually consists of a self-contained piece of work which is used to investigate a concept prior to any formal exposition. In many cases, it takes up an idea raised in a discussion point, examining it in more detail and preparing the way for formal treatment. There are also **extension tasksheets** (labelled by an E) for higher attaining students which investigate a topic in more depth and **supplementary tasksheets** (labelled by an S) which are intended to help students with a relatively weak background in a particular topic. Commentaries for all the tasksheets are included in this unit guide.

The aim of the **exercises** is to check full understanding of principles and give the student confidence through reinforcement of his or her understanding.

Graphic calculators/microcomputers are used throughout the course. In particular, much use is made of graph plotters. The use of videos and equipment for practical work is also recommended.

As well as the textbooks and unit guides, there is a *Teacher's resource file*. This file contains:

- review sheets which may be used for homework or tests;

- datasheets;

- technology datasheets which give help with using particular calculators or pieces of software;

- a programme of worksheets for more able students which would, in particular, help prepare them for the STEP examination.

Introduction to the unit (for the teacher)

The work of the seventeenth-century mathematician Galileo Galilei on projectiles and of Isaac Newton on planetary motion played a major part in the development of modern ideas on mechanics. These two areas of application of mathematics have corresponding importance in this unit. The first four chapters use the concepts mastered in *Newton's laws of motion* to study projectiles, forces, circular motion with constant speed and the statics of rigid bodies.

The concept of vector acceleration is dealt with in such a way that the many misconceptions associated with this concept are fully explored. Students acquire a sound understanding of acceleration as a vector and of Newton's second law as a vector equation, $\mathbf{F} = m\mathbf{a}$.

Throughout the unit great emphasis is placed on using and applying mathematics in real situations. Ideas for extended investigations are provided at the end of each of the first four chapters and the last chapter gives general guidance.

Using this unit

The practical tasksheets are essential. They form an integral part of the learning process and will enable the students to develop a deeper understanding of mechanics. Even if the students think that they know what will happen because of their prior knowledge of the theory, they must test whether theory and practice agree and be able to explain any discrepancies that occur. They will find that the practice gained through the tasksheets will help them design and carry out any practical experiments needed in their own extended investigations.

Good results can be obtained if care is taken but there will obviously be some discrepancy between the actual and expected results. However, this does not mean that the experiment has not succeeded. It will provide a focus for discussion and will enable the students to understand what the theory tells them. The discussion points in the last section of each chapter should not be rushed. They give the main opportunities for students to look at ideas for their extended investigations and while they will not want to make a final choice here, they should be encouraged to discuss possible topics.

Some additional notes on the individual chapters may prove helpful.

1.2 Motion under gravity

(a) Imagine that you are asked to design a stunt like the one illustrated above. Estimate how fast Eddie Kidd's bike should go to clear 20 buses.

(b) What can you say about its velocity on landing?

(c) What other mathematical questions might you ask which would help you plan the stunt successfully?

(a) Estimates between 80 and 160 km h^{-1} are reasonable.

(b) The velocity on landing might be substantially less than that at take-off if the air resistance is taken into account.

(c) Good planning would require the calculation of a safe take-off angle for the ramp. You would also need to allow sufficient space on the landing ramp and beyond for Eddie to bring the machine safely to a stop. This would depend both on his speed at take-off and the angle of the landing ramp, as well as on the friction between the ramp and the tyres.

1.3 Velocity

(a) Explain why $\mathbf{v} = \begin{bmatrix} \dfrac{dx}{dt} \\ \dfrac{dy}{dt} \end{bmatrix}$.

(b) Hence find $\mathbf{v}$ for $\mathbf{r} = \begin{bmatrix} 30t \\ 9t - 5t^2 \end{bmatrix}$.

(c) Calculate $\mathbf{v}$ when $t = 0.7, 0.9$ and 1.1 seconds.

(d) What is Eddie's speed when he lands?

(e) Interpret and validate your solutions.

(a) $\mathbf{v} = \dfrac{d\mathbf{r}}{dt}$ and for small dt, $d\mathbf{r} = \begin{bmatrix} dx \\ dy \end{bmatrix}$, so $\dfrac{d\mathbf{r}}{dt} = \begin{bmatrix} \dfrac{dx}{dt} \\ \dfrac{dy}{dt} \end{bmatrix}$

(b) If $\mathbf{r} = \begin{bmatrix} 30t \\ 9t - 5t^2 \end{bmatrix}$, $\mathbf{v} = \begin{bmatrix} 30 \\ 9 - 10t \end{bmatrix}$

(c) $\mathbf{v}(0.7) = \begin{bmatrix} 30 \\ 2 \end{bmatrix}$, $\mathbf{v}(0.9) = \begin{bmatrix} 30 \\ 0 \end{bmatrix}$, $\mathbf{v}(1.1) = \begin{bmatrix} 30 \\ -2 \end{bmatrix}$

(d) Eddie lands when $t = 1.8$ and $\mathbf{v}(1.8) = \begin{bmatrix} 30 \\ -9 \end{bmatrix}$ so his speed is
$\sqrt{(30^2 + 9^2)} = 31.3\,\mathrm{m\,s^{-1}}$.

(e) This can be interpreted as follows:

His take-off speed and landing speed are the same, that is
$31.3\,\mathrm{m\,s^{-1}} = 113\,\mathrm{km\,h^{-1}}$. The horizontal component of velocity
is always the same, $30\,\mathrm{m\,s^{-1}}$, but the vertical component is
steadily decreasing from $9\,\mathrm{m\,s^{-1}}$ on take-off, to zero after
0.9 seconds, to $-9\,\mathrm{m\,s^{-1}}$ on landing.

In the absence of any real data on speeds and velocities, these
results are validated simply by common sense. $113\,\mathrm{km\,h^{-1}}$ is a
reasonable speed. You can expect the vertical component of
velocity to decrease because of the weight. The effect of air
resistance seems to have been negligible in the 1.8 seconds of
the flight. However, the actual motion could be studied on a
video, frame by frame.

1.4 Acceleration under a constant force

(a) From the equation

force × time = change in momentum

explain how to obtain the alternative form of Newton's
second law:

force = mass × acceleration

(b) Hence explain the connection between the acceleration of
a projectile and g (the gravitational force per unit mass).

(a) Force × time = change in momentum, $\mathbf{F}t = m\mathbf{v} - m\mathbf{u}$

$\Rightarrow$ Force $= \dfrac{\text{change in momentum}}{\text{time}}$ $\mathbf{F} = \dfrac{m\mathbf{v} - m\mathbf{u}}{t}$

$= \text{mass} \times \dfrac{\text{change in velocity}}{\text{time}}$ $= m\left(\dfrac{\mathbf{v} - \mathbf{u}}{t}\right)$

$= \text{mass} \times \text{acceleration}$ $= m\mathbf{a}.$

Jumping buses

This practical should give you a feel for the factors which affect the flight of a projectile. You should quickly discover that both the angle of projection and the speed of projection will affect its path. Ensure that you only alter one variable at a time and record your results systematically.

1 You should be able to hit the target consistently. Obviously, pinpoint accuracy is not achievable, but with practice it should be possible to hit a target the size of a plate at a distance of between one and two metres.

2 The vertical height may be easier to measure accurately if you determine from what height you must fire the band in order to reach the ceiling.

3 The angle of elevation, i.e. the angle with the horizontal, can be measured with a protractor. To obtain the speed of projection, the theory from chapter 5 of *Newton's laws of motion* can be used. A body of mass one kilogram, falling under gravity, changes its momentum by $9.8\,\mathrm{kg\,m\,s^{-1}}$ in each second.

If an object is fired vertically upwards and reaches a height of one metre, for example, then the gradient of the graph of velocity against time is -9.8.

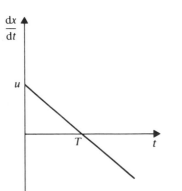

Let the initial velocity be $u\,\mathrm{m\,s^{-1}}$ vertically upwards and the highest point be reached at time T seconds. Then

$$\frac{\mathrm{d}x}{\mathrm{d}t} = u - 9.8t \quad \text{and} \quad 0 = u - 9.8T$$

The area under the graph represents the displacement, so as the band reaches a height of one metre

$$1 = \frac{1}{2}uT = \frac{1}{2}u\,\frac{u}{9.8}$$

and hence $u^2 = 19.6$

4 (a) The range (the horizontal distance between the point of projection and the point where the band lands) will be a maximum when the angle of projection is $45°$. (This may not be true in practice.)

   (b) The maximum height (and minimum range) will occur when the angle of projection is $90°$.

   (c) The time in the air is difficult to measure as the times are small. However, it is fairly easy to see that as the angle of projection decreases so does the time in the air.

Projectile motion

1 Given $\mathbf{v}(t) = \begin{bmatrix} 3.81 \\ 2.2 - 9.8t \end{bmatrix}$

then $\mathbf{r}(t) = \begin{bmatrix} 3.81t + c_1 \\ 2.2t - 4.9t^2 + c_2 \end{bmatrix}$

But $\mathbf{r}(0) = \begin{bmatrix} 0 \\ 0 \end{bmatrix} \Rightarrow c_1 = c_2 = 0$

So $\mathbf{r}(t) = \begin{bmatrix} 3.81t \\ 2.2t - 4.9t^2 \end{bmatrix}$

2 (a) $(2.2 - 4.9t)t = 0$

$\Rightarrow t = 0 \text{ or } t = \dfrac{2.2}{4.9} = 0.45$

When $t = 0.45$, $\mathbf{r}(t) = \begin{bmatrix} 3.81 \times 0.45 \\ 0 \end{bmatrix}$

$= \begin{bmatrix} 1.71 \\ 0 \end{bmatrix}$

(b) So the range is $R = 1.71$ metres.

3 You can conclude that the elastic band will land about 170 cm away, after about 0.45 seconds. During flight its highest point is about 25 cm off the ground.

4 It is clear that there is a degree of inaccuracy in these predictions. Problems arise because it is very difficult to measure accurately less than one second even with a stopwatch.

It is possible to measure the range (or even the height) and so validate the theory. Sources of error are:

- the point of projection may not be exactly at the end of the table;
- the angle of projection may not be exactly 30°;
- the velocity of projection will not be exactly $4.4 \, \text{m s}^{-1}$.

2 Statement 2 can be validated in a similar way to statement 1. In both (a) and (b) the systems of forces are in equilibrium. Scale drawing of the vectors concerned will show that they combine to give zero. Note that in validating statement 1 with apparatus (a) the forces needed to produce a given extension in an elastic band are equated. In validating statement 2 the same apparatus is used to show that as the force in the elastic band is equal in magnitude and opposite in direction to the force given on the single newton meter, the three forces (those produced by the elastic band and the two newton meters) will add up to zero.

3 The apparatus in the third experiment can be used to validate statement 3. The magnitudes and directions of the forces exerted by the four newton meters when the strings are in equilibrium can be noted. The hypothesis that they can be added by drawing a vector polygon can be validated by showing that there is a quadrilateral whose sides represent the four forces in both magnitude and direction. Note that the order of the sides of the quadrilateral will not affect this hypothesis. Care must be taken with the initialisation of the newton meters when used horizontally.

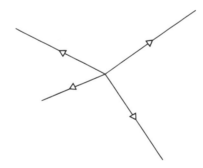

Any order can be used:

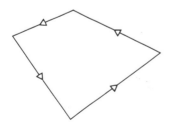   or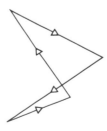

Curling

1   A suitable value of u of the first 20 metres is the average speed $\dfrac{20}{11.9} = 1.68\,\mathrm{m\,s^{-1}}$.

2   (a) For the first few seconds, the standard model $F = 0$ provides a good fit to the experimental data and is therefore satisfactory.

   (b) For $t > 10$ seconds, the model is not satisfactory and must be modified.

3   (a) Using a graphic calculator a curve can be fitted to the data. A reasonable fit is obtained by using the curve $x = 2.05t - 0.03t^2$. Hence a value of 0.06 for $\dfrac{F}{m}$ would appear to give a good model. It is interesting to note that the estimated initial speed of the stone is greater in this model than in the simple model.

3 Acceleration and circular motion

3.1 The motion of the Moon

> What force is acting on the Moon?
> What does this tell you about the direction of its acceleration?
> In what direction is the Moon travelling?
> Is its velocity changing? What about its acceleration?

The Moon experiences many forces due to its attraction by the other bodies in the solar system. The discussion should be limited initially to the force of attraction between the Moon and the Earth. This force, as with all gravitational attraction, acts along the line of centres of the two bodies. As the Moon's orbit around the Earth is nearly circular and the masses of the two bodies can be taken as constant, the magnitude of the force is approximately $2.0 \times 10^{20}\,\text{N}$. This is calculated in exercise 1.

As the force acts towards the Earth, the acceleration of the Moon is also towards the Earth. The direction of travel of the Moon is perpendicular to its acceleration. As the Moon does not disappear into deep space or crash into the Earth and always appears to be approximately the same size when seen from Earth it is reasonable to assume that it is travelling in a circle about the Earth.

As the Moon travels round the Earth the direction of the line of centres changes. Thus the directions of both the velocity and the acceleration change. As both velocity and acceleration are vectors they therefore change in direction but not magnitude.

3.4 Acceleration

> The car described above completes a lap of the track at a speed of $2\,\text{m s}^{-1}$.
>
> (a) How does its velocity change as it goes round the track?
>
> (b) How does its acceleration change? Calculate the maximum and minimum acceleration.

(a) The velocity is constant on all the straight sections, as both speed and direction are constant. However, on the bends, the velocity at any point is perpendicular to the radius of the bend and so its direction is changing there. The magnitude of the velocity remains constant.

(b) The acceleration is zero on the straight sections. On the bends the acceleration is radially inwards.

Where $r = 30\,cm = 0.3\,m$, the acceleration is about $13\,m\,s^{-2}$.
Where $r = 50\,cm = 0.5\,m$, the acceleration is about $8\,m\,s^{-2}$.

The maximum acceleration is therefore $13\,m\,s^{-2}$ and the minimum acceleration is zero.

3.5 Modelling with circular motion

Describe the motion in each of the situations above.
What assumptions should you make in each case?
How valid are your assumptions?

What other situations can you think of which might be modelled using the mechanics in this chapter?

The wall of death (or the rotor)

People stand at the edge of a large cylindrical drum. This starts to rotate, slowly at first and then faster and faster. The people rotate with the drum, carried round by the friction between themselves and the floor and walls of the drum. Once the motion has attained a certain speed, the floor is lowered and the people find themselves flattened against the walls of the drum with no apparent means of support. However, it is vital that the floor should be replaced before the drum is brought to rest or the people will fall to the bottom.

In order to study this phenomenon the following assumptions should be made:

- The people are particles of given mass.

- The coefficient of friction between the people and the drum is constant.

- The drum is rotating at constant speed and has constant radius.

- Air resistance can be ignored and $g = 9.8\,m\,s^{-2}$.

These assumptions are sufficient to give an initial analysis of the motion, but for a full analysis the motion should be studied during the process of starting and stopping the ride. The effect of variation in the coefficient of friction could also be studied.

Investigating angular speed

The choice of practical will depend on the apparatus available. A simple turntable can be made by fixing a cardboard disc with a hole in the centre to a pulley and clampstand using double-sided sticky tape or Blu-Tack. A length of string can be placed round the pulley and used to drive the turntable. The pulleys from the 16–19 mechanics kit have a 1 cm radius so that pulling the string at $2\,\text{cm}\,\text{s}^{-1}$ will enable the disc to be turned at an angular speed of 2 radians per second.

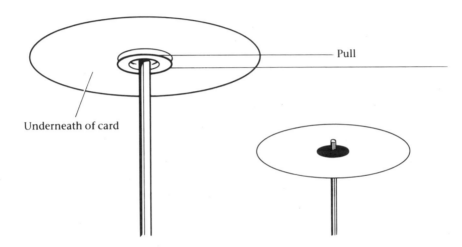

Pull

Underneath of card

Alternatively a motor driven turntable can be used if available. The plastic strips from the 16–19 mechanics kits can be cut to give three sets of apparatus for version 2.

The answers for the questions are similar whichever apparatus is used.

1   The angular speed is 2 radians per second.

The angular speed in r.p.m. is $\dfrac{2 \times 60}{2\pi} = 19.1$ r.p.m. to 3 s.f.

2 $v = \omega r$
$v = 2 \times 0.06\,\text{m}\,\text{s}^{-1}$
$\quad = 0.12\,\text{m}\,\text{s}^{-1}$

Note that ω must be measured in $\text{rad}\,\text{s}^{-1}$.

3   The velocity of the penny is $0.12\,\text{m}\,\text{s}^{-1}$ tangentially.

4   (a)   If the speed is to be half that of the first penny then $v = 0.06$.
ω is constant no matter where the penny is, so $0.06 = 2r$, hence $r = 0.03$ metres.
The penny must be 3 cm from the centre. (In the case of the pencil point it can be 0.3 cm either side of the centre.)

(b) The penny must be anywhere on the disc 12 cm from the centre.

(c) The directions of motion must be the same so the penny must lie 12 cm from the centre on the line joining the centre of the turntable to the centre of the penny.

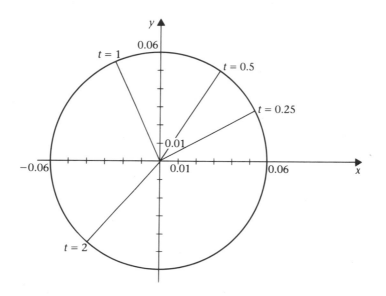

5 The turntable has turned through $\frac{1}{2}\pi$ rad so the time taken is
$$\frac{\frac{1}{2}\pi}{2} = 0.785 \text{ seconds to 3 s.f.}$$

6

t	0	0.25	0.5	1	2
$\mathbf{r}$	$\begin{bmatrix} 0.06 \\ 0.00 \end{bmatrix}$	$\begin{bmatrix} 0.05 \\ 0.033 \end{bmatrix}$	$\begin{bmatrix} 0.033 \\ 0.05 \end{bmatrix}$	$\begin{bmatrix} -0.025 \\ 0.055 \end{bmatrix}$	$\begin{bmatrix} -0.04 \\ -0.045 \end{bmatrix}$

7 The coordinates after t seconds are $\mathbf{r} = 0.06 \begin{bmatrix} \cos 2t \\ \sin 2t \end{bmatrix}$.

Satellites

1

Possible assumptions are:

- The Earth is a perfect sphere of mass 5.973×10^{24} kg and radius 6378 km.

- The gravitational constant is 6.673×10^{-11}.

- The astronaut travels in a perfectly circular orbit $(467 + 6378)$ km above the centre of the Earth.

- The astronaut is a particle of mass m kg and his speed is constant, v m s^{-1}.

- The force of attraction of the Earth on George Nelson is R newtons towards the centre of the Earth.

- The satellite travels from west to east above the equator. (You might choose east to west.)

2 Using Newton's law of gravitation

$$R = \frac{5.973 \times 6.673 \times 10^{13} \times m}{10^{12} \times 6.845^2} = 8.507\,m \text{ newtons}$$

But by Newton's second law, as the astronaut is travelling in a circle at constant speed v:

$$8.507\,m = \frac{mv^2}{6.845 \times 10^6}$$

$$v^2 = 58\,230\,000$$
$$v = 7631\,\text{m s}^{-1}$$

The angular speed of the astronaut is $\dfrac{v}{r}$ or $\dfrac{7631}{6\,378\,000}$ rad s^{-1}

so one complete revolution takes 5236 seconds or 1.454 hours.

So in 24 hours the astronaut rotates 16.5 times around the centre of the Earth. If he travels in the same direction as the Earth, i.e. west to east, then he will travel over Singapore 15 more times in the next 24 hours. If, however, the satellite travels in the opposite direction, east to west, then he will pass over Singapore 17 more times.

4 Rigid bodies

4.1 Rotating objects

> (a) Watch from the side as one person throws a tennis racket through the air to another person, as shown in the picture above. Describe its path. Does it behave like a projectile?
>
> (b) Stick a red dot on the side of the handle and watch the dot as the racket is thrown. Describe the path of the red dot.
>
> (c) Balance the racket horizontally on your finger and place the dot at the balance point. Describe the path of the red dot in this case.
>
> (d) Can you suggest some rules for how any rigid body moves through the air when thrown?

(a) You would expect a projectile to follow a parabolic path, but the rotation of the tennis racket makes it difficult to see if this is in fact what happens.

(b) The path of the red dot will look something like this:

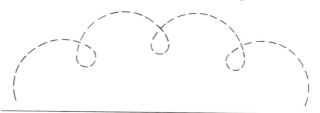

(c) The path of the red dot now appears to follow a simple parabola.

(d) Below are just some of the rules that may have been suggested during the discussion.

- A rigid body will usually rotate when thrown.

- When viewed from a distance the rotation will not be noticeable and the rigid body will look like a particle following a parabolic path.

- If you can find a 'balance' point then this point seems to act as a centre for the rotation of the body.

- The balance point seems to be following a parabolic path when the body is thrown.

Which slides first?

Problem

Which finger slides first?

Set up a model

Assume that the track is uniform and of mass M and is held horizontally in equilibrium on two fingers at A and B.
Let each finger exert a normal force N_a and N_b.
Assume that the finger at A is further away from the centre of the track and that the coefficient of friction is the same for each finger.
Let the friction due to the push of each finger on the track be P inwards.

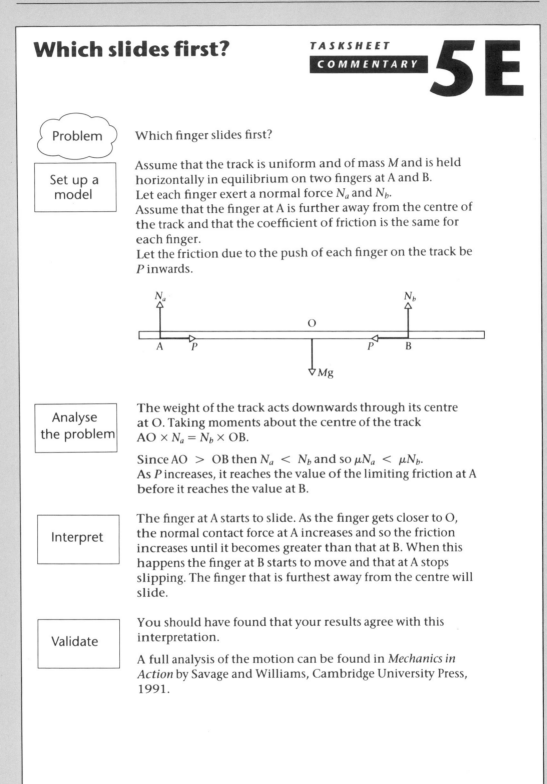

Analyse the problem

The weight of the track acts downwards through its centre at O. Taking moments about the centre of the track
$$AO \times N_a = N_b \times OB.$$

Since $AO > OB$ then $N_a < N_b$ and so $\mu N_a < \mu N_b$.
As P increases, it reaches the value of the limiting friction at A before it reaches the value at B.

Interpret

The finger at A starts to slide. As the finger gets closer to O, the normal contact force at A increases and so the friction increases until it becomes greater than that at B. When this happens the finger at B starts to move and that at A stops slipping. The finger that is furthest away from the centre will slide.

Validate

You should have found that your results agree with this interpretation.

A full analysis of the motion can be found in *Mechanics in Action* by Savage and Williams, Cambridge University Press, 1991.